Scott Foresman

Readers' Theater
Anthology

PEARSON

Scott
Foresman

Editorial Offices: Glenview, Illinois • Parsippany, New Jersey • New York, New York
Sales Offices: Needham, Massachusetts • Duluth, Georgia • Glenview, Illinois
Coppell, Texas • Sacramento, California • Mesa, Arizona

Grade 3

Reading STREET

Acknowledgments

Poetry

P5 "Lunch Money," from *Lunch Money* by Carol Diggory Shields, copyright © 1995 by Carol Diggory Shields, text. Used by permission of Dutton Children's Books, A Division of Penguin Young Readers Group, A Member of Penguin Group (USA) Inc., 345 Hudson Street, New York, NY 10014. All rights reserved.

P6 "How to Eat a Sandwich Cookie" by Beverly McLoughland from *Yummy! Eating Through a Day*, edited by Lee Bennett Hopkins. Copyright © 2000 Simon & Schuster Books for Young Readers. Used by permission of the author, who controls all rights.

P7 "Meeting the Snake" by Tony Mitton from *Reptile Poems*, edited by John Foster. Copyright © 1996 Oxford University Press. Used by permission of David Higham Associates.

P7 "The Porcupine" by Karla Kuskin. Copyright © 1975 by Karla Kushkin. Reprinted by permission of Scott Freimel NY.

P8 "Good Morning" by Muriel Sipe from *Sung Under the Silver Umbrella*. Used by permission of the Association for Childhood Education International.

P9 "I Like Myself!" text copyright © 2004 by Karen Beaumont, reprinted by permission of Harcourt, Inc.

P11 "Foreign Fare" from *Stepping Out with Grandma Mae* by Nikki Grimes. Published by Orchard Books/Scholastic Inc. Copyright © 2001 by Nikki Grimes. Reprinted by permission of Scholastic Inc.

P12 "A Lion," copyright © 1994 by Romana Bass & Arnold Rampersad, Administrators of the Estate of Langston Hughes, from *The Sweet and Sour Animal Book* by Langston Hughes. Used by permission of Oxford University Press, Inc.

P12 "Freedom Is . . ." by Clarie Grierson from *Breaking Free: An Anthology of Human Rights Poetry*, selected by Robert Hull, 1944, Wayland Publishers, Ltd.

P13 "At the Library" copyright © 1997 by Nikki Grimes. First appeared in *It's Raining Laughter*, published by Dial Books for Young Readers. Reprinted by permission of Curtis Brown, Ltd.

P15 "My Brother Is as Generous as Anyone Could Be" by Jack Prelutsky. Text copyright © 1990 by Jack Prelutsky. Used by permission of HarperCollins Publishers.

ISBN: 0-328-14731-1

Copyright © Pearson Education, Inc.

13 14 15 VON4 13 12

Contents

Practice with a Purpose

by Sam Sebesta

As indicated in the directions in this book, Readers' Theater is a performance activity with a simple format. Costumes, makeup, and scenery are not required. Action is minimal. Because scripts are used, there's no lengthy time spent memorizing lines.

The goal is a shared oral reading performance that rocks the rafters, whether an audience is present or not. People with long memories compare it to radio drama in days of old. Yet there's nothing out-of-date about Readers' Theater. Its benefits are recognized by modern researchers. Listen to this:

TEACHER (*puzzled*): Why are we doing Readers' Theater?

READING PROFESSOR (*reading from a scholarly paper*): "Readers' Theater promotes fluency and expression as a result of repeated reading and encouragement to make the performance sound natural and meaningful."

STUDENT 1 (*aside*): Will that be on the test? No, that won't be on the test, although it's a good rationale for teachers to know about. Beyond this, it might be beneficial to discuss the reasons for Readers' Theater with your class.

TEACHER (*still puzzled*): Why are we doing Readers' Theater?

STUDENT 2: Because it's fun.

STUDENT 3: Because you learn to get the words right.

STUDENT 4: You learn to speak up so others can hear you.

STUDENT 5 (*the reflective one*): It's good for the imagination.

Good reasons, all. Here are five more, gleaned from comments during Readers' Theater classes and workshops:

ABOUT THE AUTHOR
Sam Sebesta is a Professor Emeritus from the College of Education at the University of Washington in Seattle. He continues to write and do research in children's literature, decoding in linguistic development, oral reading fluency, and reader response.

"You get practice with a purpose."

The purpose, of course, is to present a worthy performance. The practice? It begins the moment scripts are passed out. It continues as students take their parts home or to a quiet corner to practice their lines. It flourishes in group rehearsal.

"You learn to make it sound like people talking."

A smooth delivery—flow of language, not word-by-word—is an objective in Readers' Theater that students can understand. How to achieve it? Practice reading a line and then look up and say it directly to another character. Pretty soon the fluency will come.

"More of you get to read at one time."

In this student's class, several groups are rehearsing their scripts simultaneously before they come together to perform for each other. The ratio of readers to listeners is higher than you'd find in classes where one reads and all others listen. Hence, there's more practice, more involvement.

"You learn to get into character."

Sounds too grown-up? Not at all! Children realize, from the start, that the way to portray Chicken Little is to try running like Chicken Little and talking like Chicken Little. Using mime and made-up speeches to help "get into character" may be a useful device to prepare for Readers' Theater. And there may be a more lasting payoff: readers who enjoy reading often see themselves in the roles of the characters they're reading about.

"It's reading you get to do with your friends."

Avid readers, when interviewed, speak frequently about the social value of reading, praising reading activities that have them interacting with peers. Non-avid readers who think of reading as a lonely task may also find that interactive activities such as Readers' Theater and Choral Reading alter attitudes toward the positive.

These, then, are benefits you may discover from Readers' Theater and Choral Reading. There may be more. The effects of good oral reading may be internalized, resulting in improved silent reading. Hence, speaking and listening to complex style, dialogue in character, and other features of print contribute to effective silent reading. It's no coincidence that avid readers (i.e., children and young adults who read voluntarily an hour or more a day) cite reading aloud and being read to as the major factor leading to their success.

With all these reasons in mind, Scott Foresman Reading Street offers you the directions and selections in this book. We hope you enjoy them. We want you to find them useful as a component of a powerful reading program.

Readers' Theater in Your Classroom

by Alisha Fran-Potter

Staging the Play

ACTING AREA

If you don't have a stage at your disposal, your classroom will work fine. First you need to define a functional acting area. This could be the front or back of the room with some or all of the desks pushed out of the way. It could be a taped-off area on the floor. If you need or want to leave all your desks in place, you will need enough space in front of the room for students to stand in a row. It may take some trial and error before you decide what will work best for your class and room layout. Explain the plan to your students and train them how to prepare the acting area when you give the signal.

ABOUT THE AUTHOR

Alisha Fran-Potter is a Drama Specialist with the Glenview, Illinois, public schools. She has taught in classrooms at grades K, 1, and 2, and speech, drama, and language arts at

MOVEMENT AND BLOCKING

Traditionally, Readers' Theater is performed with the actors seated on chairs or stools in a row facing the audience, with their scripts in their hands or on stands in front of them. Actors do not memorize their parts but read them or at least refer to their scripts as they act. In this traditional method, actors do not look at each other but keep their focus out front. You can include movement in your production or not. Decide before you start how much movement there will be. Keep in mind that if students have scripts in their hands, their movements must be limited. If they remain in place, they might gesture with one free hand.

Any movement about the stage you have the actors do is called *blocking*. Your blocking choices depend on your acting area. If you have the space and want to have your actors move about freely, do so. However, if your acting area is limited, keep the blocking simple, perhaps just having the actors move from one chair to another, cross the stage, or come and go in the acting area.

If the actors are up and moving around, you need to consider their focus (whom they are talking to), and angle (the direction they face). Actors should not face each other directly, but rather turn their bodies slightly toward the audience. This is called *cheating*, and if done well it can look perfectly natural. In cheating positions, two actors would position their bodies at about 90° to each other.

If there is a place that remains the same throughout the story, such as a house or a lake, you might tape an area out on the floor or block it off with chairs or markers. This way all actors know where the place is within the acting area. You can designate entrances and exits in the same way.

ENTRANCES AND EXITS

For a smooth-running performance, rehearse entrances and exits when you rehearse the play.

- Actors can all enter at the same time, go to their assigned places, and then all exit at the same time. Or, they can all be "discovered" by lights up at the beginning—with lights down to signal the end.

- Actors can enter as their characters come into the story and then stay or leave and come back. You will need to decide if all the actors stay on stage after their parts are finished. (If they remain, they can all share a curtain call.)

- Actors can remain at their desks until it is their turn to perform, do their roles, and then go back to their seats. This works only if your classroom is big enough to accommodate a seating area and separate acting area.

ASSIGNING PARTS

Plan in advance how parts will be assigned and explain the process to your students. Some ways to do this are:

Volunteers This method allows students to volunteer for the parts they are interested in. Go though all the parts and describe them if necessary. Then explain that when you ask who is interested in playing each part they should raise their hands. Suggest that students have second and third choices in mind because they won't always get their first choices. If you know that a volunteer can't handle a specific part for whatever reason, choose another student and give the first student a more appropriate part. This works better with some groups than with other groups, and you must assess your students' abilities to handle volunteering.

Draw Markers To assign parts randomly, make up sticks with the student's names on them. Choose a stick and assign that person the part that is up next. This works well if all the parts are about the same in length and difficulty—and if the parts are gender-neutral. You will have to use your discretion, however, to avoid choosing a student who can't handle the reading of a role because it is large or because it will embarrass the student for some reason.

Teacher Choice Do this ahead of time to save class time. Simply go through the cast list and the student list and decide who will play what part. This works well—and indeed may be necessary—if there are varied abilities in the class and the roles vary much in length. But you must know your students and the parts in the play well in order to use this method.

SCENERY AND PROPS

Scenery provides the *setting*—where the story takes place. If you have access to a curtain backdrop, use it by all means. Chances are, however, that you are stuck with a wall of your classroom. If you have the space, you might be able to arrange desks, tables, carts, easels, chairs, and so on to suggest a setting. You might consider having students create a scene in colored chalk on your chalkboard. Keep in mind, however, that the best scenery is created in the imaginations of your audience.

Props are anything the actors handle. Traditional Readers' Theater uses no props, but if you choose to use props, keep them simple. Remember that the actors still have to manipulate their scripts. If the play calls for a bag or a purse, the actor can use a backpack or coat. Other ordinary classroom items that can serve as props include: books, clipboards, pencil cases, boxes, book ends, pens or pencils, paper, note cards, notebooks, cups, vases, water bottles.

Adapting Scripts

Ideally, every student in a class or group will have his or her own role in Readers' Theater. If these scripts have too many or too few roles for your class, you may need to adapt them to fit. To reduce characters:

- Eliminate parts that are redundant or not vital to the plot. For example, reduce four narrators to two by having Narrator 1 read lines designated Narrator 1 and Narrator 3, and so on.

- Take out parts with animal sounds or cheering crowds and just let the audience infer them.

- Characters with single lines or few lines can be doubled by actors who aren't in the same scene.

- Perform only scenes for which you have enough actors. You can summarize or narrate missing scenes that are needed to get the story across.

To add characters:

- If there are many Narrator lines, divide them up to allow for more narrators.
- Have two students play a role at the same time. If there is a cat in the story, turn it into two cats. They can alternate lines or recite them in unison.
- Add a counterpart character and have them say their lines together or divide the lines. For example, if there is a Queen in the story, create a King.
- If there is a part such as Townsperson, turn it into Townspeople and have more than one actor read it simultaneously.
- If many extra parts are needed, cast by scene. For example, have different actors play the King in Scene 1 and Scene 2.

Note that the suggestions for simultaneous reading also work well to help students with special needs or ELL students who are just learning English.

Adapting Trade Books for Readers' Theater

You can adapt any kind of book into a Readers' Theater script. But not every story is equally suited to the stage. Look for a story with a strong narrative line. An easy-to-follow plot adapts more effectively than a plot or story line that is too complex. If it feels complicated, you might need to simplify the plot somehow. Even nonfiction books can be turned into scripts, but among those, the books with strong narrative lines—such as biography or history—will be most effective. Here are some further elements to consider:

Narration When you are adapting your script, first eliminate all speech tags, such as "he said" and "Josefina replied." Eliminate lengthy descriptions. If you feel some description is necessary, try to put it in the mouth of a character who has a reason to describe something.

Narrators can be very useful, but try to keep their function to introducing or summarizing the story. Sometimes they may be necessary to make transitions between scenes. However, don't rely on narrators to tell the story. For example, don't write:

NARRATOR: It is early Monday morning. Mary is eagerly waiting for friends to look at her garden before the judges come. Finally Tessa arrives.

MARY: I'll show you my flowers.

NARRATOR: Together they walk to the garden in back of the house. They see beautiful bright yellow sunflowers and blazing red poppies.

Aim to show, not to tell. In other words, dramatize, don't narrate. For example, you might write:

NARRATOR: It is early Monday morning. Mary is eagerly waiting.

MARY: Good morning, Tessa!

TESSA: Hi, Mary. I've come to see that award-winning garden of yours.

MARY: I hope. But I'm glad you could come before the judges get here.

TESSA: So am I. I can't wait to see what you've done this year. I hear it's beautiful and full of color.

MARY: Oh, it is! I have bright yellow sunflowers and blazing red poppies. Here, let me show you. It's out back. Follow me.

You will find that it is helpful to have characters repeat each other's names often. This helps the audience (and the actors) keep track of who is speaking, especially when there are a lot of characters in a scene.

Dialogue Look at the dialogue in a book to see how much there is. Some dialogue you might be able to use directly in your script. Some you may need to simplify or pare down. Some dialogue you may decide to break up into smaller units, so that one character doesn't talk for too long at one time.

Be sure that the dialogue is appropriate for the age group you're working with. If not, you may be able to make it more appropriate by cutting or substituting some words or phrases.

Repetition Repetition may be of actions or of language. Repetition of actions allows actors—and the audience—to follow the story line more easily. For example, the First Pig builds a house of straw, the Second Pig builds a house of twigs, and the Third Pig builds a house of bricks.

Repetition of language might be a repeated phrase or sentence such as the Wolf's line, "I'll huff and I'll puff and I'll blow your house down!" which he says before his attack on each Pig's house.

Younger children especially do well with repetition. But many folk tales appropriate to higher levels also develop their plot lines through the use of repetition.

Group Characters These allow for multiple roles. For example, if you have twenty-six actors with one main character and five supporting characters, all can have a role. One or two actors can play the main character, and then several actors can play each of the supporting characters. For example, take the story *Anansi and the Moss-Covered Rock* by Eric Kimmel.

Anansi, the spider, is walking though the forest when he finds a magic rock. He uses this rock to trick his friends so he can take their food. Little Bush Deer won't let Anansi fool him, though, and teaches Anansi a lesson in turn.

One or two actors can play Anansi, one or two can play the rock, and the rest of the actors can be divided among the other animals. So you might have three or four Lions, Elephants, Rhinoceroses, Hippopotamuses, Giraffes, Zebras, and Little Bush Deers.

Special Effects

You can create effective Readers' Theater using nothing but the actors' voices. However, if you want to add to the theatrical experience, consider the following:

MUSIC

You can use recorded or live music (such as a piano or guitar) to make transitions between scenes, to show the passage of time, or for background to heighten the mood. Be sure that the music is appropriate to the mood and pace of the scene. If you are using recorded music, practice cueing it up during rehearsals.

LIGHTING

If you are working on a stage with a lighting system, you can either open the curtain or bring the lights up on your actors already in place. If the actors must take their places in view of the audience, you can dim the lights to black and then bring them up to signal the start of the performance.

SOUND EFFECTS

Remember that the actors themselves can create all the sound effects with their voices alone. However, here are some additional suggestions for these plays.

When Your Feet Can Reach the Pedals The sound of Matt's dropping an armload of rocks could be achieved by dumping a box full of any number of objects. Let students experiment for the most satisfying crash sounds.

The Pied Piper of Hamelin Students can make rat and cat noises verbally—whatever howls and hisses they can contrive. For the piper's music, a whistle or flute would be ideal. If that is not possible, you can play brief excerpts of recorded music or some flute-like runs on a piano. Or, a talented student whistler could supply the music.

Rescue the Pufflings! Students' ad-lib bird calls may sound more like crows than seagulls and puffins. No matter; the effect to achieve is a brief wash of wild bird noises.

About the Playwrights

Jim Hughes is a Professor Emeritus at Oakland (CA) University's School of Education. He also worked on education projects in Kenya, Nepal, Indonesia, Yemen Arab Republic, and Pakistan. He is co-author of twenty-one texts in elementary social studies. He is also a published playwright in musical theatre, and his plays have been produced in regional theatres in New Mexico, California, and Colorado. Currently he is working on the books and lyrics for several musicals.

Judy Freed wrote the children's musical *Tickle Cakes*, which has toured three states and was recognized by the American Alliance for Theatre & Education. Her musical *Tantrum on the Tracks* was commissioned by the Duncan YMCA of Chicago. Adult musicals include *Emma & Company; Me and Al*, which was showcased at the International Festival of Musical Theatre in Cardiff, Wales; and *Sleepy Hollow*, which was developed at the ASCAP/Disney Musical Theater Workshop.

Don Abramson wrote *Melissa, While She Sleeps*, a collection of poems that was staged in Phoenix, Chicago, New York, and London, England. He has written several short plays for children that were published in reading textbooks. He wrote the books and lyrics for two children's musicals, *The Well of the Guelphs*, which was produced in Lincoln, Nebraska, and Okoboji, Iowa, and *Who Is Cinderella?* which was commissioned by Chicago's Duncan YMCA.

Amy Fellner Dominy writes for both children's theater and adult theater. She studied creative writing at Arizona State University. A number of her plays have had readings or productions, among them *The Bathtub, The Dreamcatcher, Oy! It's a Boy, Folding Memories, Some Assembly Required,* and *Plastic Angels.* She is a member of The Dramatists Guild, the Society of Children's Book Writers, and the Association of Jewish Theatre.

Laurel Haines writes plays and musicals and also enjoys directing and acting. Her plays for young audiences include *Stones of Wisdom*, a puppet musical produced by First Stage Children's Theater at the 2003 Milwaukee Summer Fest. Some of her other produced plays include *Tales from the Crib, Raw Footage*, and *A Ton of Feathers*. Her play *The Dianalogues* was published in *Women Playwrights: The Best Plays of 2003.*

Alisha Fran-Potter is a Drama Specialist with Glenview (IL) School District 34. She has taught Kindergarten, 1st and 2nd grade, Drama for grades K–8, and Drama and Speech for grades 6–8. Mrs. Fran-Potter developed, wrote, and implemented fine arts curriculums for Districts 34 and 81. She has presented at the Illinois Reading Council and taught for Glenview University.

To create the script for "What Does Freedom Mean?" she asked a number of third-grade students (Mrs. Mascari's class) from Hoffman School in Glenview to interview family members and other elders on that question. The students wrote scenes and combined them under Mrs. Fran-Potter's guidance. Finally, she polished the script and edited it for length.

WHEN YOUR FEET CAN REACH

THE PEDALS

By Jim Hughes

KIDS LEARN THAT GETTING MONEY TO BUY
SOMETHING THEY WANT MAY NOT BE AS SIMPLE
AS ASKING MOM OR DAD FOR IT.

CHARACTERS

JOHNNY RYAN (9 years)
DONNA (8 years)
JAKE (8 years)
WENDY (10 years)
FREDDIE (8 years)
MATT (9 years)
DEBORAH (9 years)
MRS. RYAN
MR. RYAN
MRS. DUNCAN
MRS. MYERS
MRS. PULASKI
MR. ROSENBERG
MR. DIAZ, the Principal
NARRATORS 1–2
SOUND EFFECTS

SCENE 1

MRS. RYAN Wash your hands, Johnny. Your breakfast is ready.

JOHNNY Oatmeal, ick. Any lumps?

MR. RYAN Just eat it, Johnny. Don't worry about the lumps.

JOHNNY Can I ask a favor, Dad?

MR. RYAN Try me.

JOHNNY Would you buy me an ATV?

MRS. RYAN What on earth's an ATV?

JOHNNY It's an all-terrain vehicle, Mom. A kind of car that can go anywhere off the roads.

MRS. RYAN Johnny, you're only in third grade. Those things are too dangerous.

JOHNNY A lot of kids in my class are getting them, Mom.

MR. RYAN A lot of kids in your class are spoiled.

JOHNNY When I'm in high school, would you buy me a car, Dad?

MR. RYAN When your feet can reach the pedals, we'll talk about it, Johnny.

JOHNNY Steve just got a car.

MRS. RYAN Yes, well, Johnny, your brother is eighteen. He's been working part-time bagging groceries for the past three years.

MR. RYAN And he saved his money, son.

MRS. RYAN It'll be a good many years before your feet can reach the pedals of a car. Now finish your oatmeal, Johnny, or you'll be late for school.

JOHNNY Had enough, Mom. I'd better run, or I'll miss the school bus. G'bye!

MR. AND MRS. RYAN Goodbye, Johnny.

MRS. RYAN Ned, I don't know where kids get these ideas. Johnny's only nine, and he's talking ATVs and cars. And he already has his own CD player and computer. Kids today have too many things.

MR. RYAN You know, Janis, kids just don't appreciate the value of a dollar.

MRS. RYAN Well, I'm going to do something about it, Ned. To start with, I'll call Mrs. Duncan. She's president of the Parents' Association at Johnny's school. Maybe we can organize a group of interested parents and talk about it.

NARRATOR 1 First, Mrs. Ryan called Mildred Duncan. Then she called Emily Myers, Rita Pulaski, and Arthur Rosenberg. Soon, a meeting was planned at the school.

SCENE 2

MRS. DUNCAN Order, please! We're here to talk about the kids.

MRS. MYERS Yes, our young people think we have an endless supply of money.

MRS. PULASKI My daughter wants a digital camera.

MR. ROSENBERG My kids want their own laptop computers.

MRS. DUNCAN And in the middle school they all seem to have cell phones.

MRS. MYERS Kids want to have every new gadget that comes out.

MRS. RYAN My third-grade son asked us to buy him an ATV and later, a car.

MR. RYAN We told him that when his feet can reach the pedals, we'll talk about it.

NARRATOR 2 The Parents' Association sent some parents to discuss the problem with Mr. Diaz, the principal. He listened carefully. Then he had something to say.

MR. DIAZ We need to find a way to teach the kids a lesson about money. I've got an idea. We'll create a different way of paying for things that will drive home the point. For example, we could require kids to use rocks and stones as money.

MRS. RYAN But how would that work? No store will accept that kind of money!

MR. DIAZ Here's what I'm thinking. Let's have a fair here at the school. We could call it a "Flintstones Fair," because the kids would use Stone-age money.

MR. ROSENBERG Hmmm . . . you've got my attention. Go on.

MR. DIAZ Well, suppose we offer food, beverages, and trinkets for sale at the fair. And let's say we accept only Stone-age money as payment.

MRS. DUNCAN That's an interesting idea, Mr. Diaz. But how would kids get the rocks they need to buy things with?

MRS. PULASKI I've got an idea! The teachers could give each kid an allowance of a certain number of rocks before the fair.

MR. RYAN That's good, Mrs. Pulaski. But let's teach them something about earning money, too. We could have booths where kids could do things to earn extra money—er—rocks!

MRS. PULASKI Sure! We could have them answer questions relating to their studies in class. They'd have to answer correctly, of course, to get rocks.

MRS. MYERS Even better than that—we could have kids sign up on sheets promising to give time after the fair to help clean up. They'd earn rocks for that.

MR. ROSENBERG But how will the sellers at the fair COUNT the rock money?

MR. DIAZ Well, Mr. Rosenberg, we can make up our own rules. We can give the smallest value to very tiny pebbles, then the next higher value to large pebbles.

MRS. MYERS Oh, I see, Mr. Diaz. Rocks would be worth even more, and . . . .

MRS. DUNCAN Really big rocks—boulders—would be worth the most.

MR. DIAZ You've got it. I think we should make our system as much like real money as possible. We could say that twenty-five tiny pebbles equals one large pebble.

MRS. PULASKI And four big pebbles equals one rock.

MRS. MYERS And so on up the line.

MR. ROSENBERG I think dealing with all these rocks and hauling them around just to buy things could make it hard on the kids.

MRS. DUNCAN But that's the whole point, Mr. Rosenberg. We want the kids to learn that coming up with money to buy things is not so easy.

MR. ROSENBERG Yes, I see your point, Mrs. Duncan.

MR. DIAZ So are you parents with me on this? Will you pitch in and help us do the work and raise the money?

ALL PARENTS (ad lib) Yes. You can count on us. Sure. Let's do it!

NARRATOR 1 Mr. Diaz and the parents worked hard planning the Flintstones Fair. Mr. Diaz got the teachers and custodians to go along with the plan too.

SCENE 3

NARRATOR 2 At last, the day of the fair arrived. The rules for buying things with rock money had been explained to all the kids. Every kid at the fair started out with an allowance—a pocketful of pebbles and rocks. The booths for earning and spending money were all in place in the school cafeteria.

JOHNNY Hey, Donna, what are you going to buy?

DONNA Well, I really want a bracelet I saw. But I've already spent rocks on something to eat and drink, and I don't have many left.

JOHNNY Why don't you try to earn rocks at one of the booths?

DONNA I guess I could try, Johnny. Say, what do you want to buy?

JOHNNY I want a model of an antique car that I saw.

DONNA Sounds like it costs a lot.

JOHNNY Well, I think I could get enough rocks, pebbles, and boulders. But I'm not sure I could haul them very far—without a wagon.

JAKE Hey, guys, this fair is a bust. I just tried to buy a hot dog, and the guy at the booth wouldn't take my pebbles.

JOHNNY Where did you get them from?

JAKE Ha, ha! I found them on the school ground and brought them inside.

WENDY Well, no wonder, Jake! Your rocks didn't come from inside school. They're counterfeit—as phony as you are.

FREDDIE Maybe Jake's teeny pebbles aren't any good, Wendy. But even with good pebbles and rocks, it's a pain. I tried to earn some pebbles at the question booth. I got all the questions wrong . . . and didn't earn a thing.

MATT (calling out) Heeelllpppp! I can't carry these another step farther!

FREDDIE Look! There's Matt. He's trying to carry a pile of rocks and boulders on top of that book bag.

SOUND EFFECTS Ping, ping, ping, bang, ker plunk, ker PLOHNK!

WENDY Oh no! He dropped all of them. They're scattering all over the floor.

DEBORAH I don't know about you guys, but I'm heading for the exit.

ALL STUDENTS (ad lib) Yeah, let's go. This is no fun. What a bummer!

SCENE 4

NARRATOR 1 The next couple of days, students talked about the Flintstones Fair.

DEBORAH We want real money again. Forget about those stupid rocks.

DONNA The Flintstones Fair was SUPPOSED to be fun—but it wasn't. When I want something, I ask my parents for money, and they give me REAL money.

MATT Yeah, I couldn't believe how hard it was to haul those rocks around. A lot different from cool cash!

FREDDIE Teachers gave us an allowance before the fair, but it was pretty small. I guess they knew we couldn't hold many rocks at one time. I thought earning extra pebbles at the fair was hard work, and you sure didn't get very many.

WENDY Listen to us, you guys! I think our parents and teachers were trying to teach us a lesson. We think getting something we want is as easy as asking Mom or Dad, "Hey, can I have some money?" But they have to work for the money, and it's not always so easy to earn it.

MATT You know, Wendy? You're making a lot of sense. Maybe when we want something extra expensive—like a laptop or a TV—we should try to take on extra chores. Maybe our parents would agree to help us out.

NARRATOR 2 All the kids agreed they would go home and talk to their parents about the Flintstones Fair and what they'd learned.

SCENE 5

NARRATOR 1 At the Ryan dinner table, conversation went like this.

MR. RYAN Johnny, you haven't said much about the Flintstones Fair at school. Did you like it? Did you and your friends have fun?

JOHNNY Gee, Dad. It was weird. Getting enough rocks together to buy anything was tough. And it was REALLY hard to haul the rocks you needed to buy something big. I'm glad we use paper money and coins in real stores!

MRS. RYAN (chuckling) We thought you'd discover that using rocks for money isn't so terrific. You know, Johnny, people in different times and places have used all kinds of things for money. But we have a system that works pretty well.

JOHNNY Well, there's one other thing, Mom and Dad.

MR. RYAN What's that, Johnny?

JOHNNY We kids ask for money an awful lot. I guess we didn't realize how hard it is to earn. I was thinking . . . .

MRS. RYAN Yes Johnny?

JOHNNY Maybe when I want to buy something big—well, maybe I could do extra chores to earn money. Maybe you could help me save it too.

MRS. RYAN Johnny, that sounds like a good idea. I think your dad and I could work something out with you. Right, Honey?

MR. RYAN Definitely. You're on the right track, son. Say, do you still want that car you asked about?

JOHNNY Dad, I think I can wait 'til my feet can reach the pedals.

The Pied Piper

of Hamelin

based on an old
German legend

by Judy Freed

*The people of Hamelin learn to keep
their promises, but only after losing
what they cherish most.*

CHARACTERS

ANNA
HANS
SOFIE
ANNA'S MOTHER
ANNA'S FATHER
HANS'S MOTHER
HANS'S FATHER
SOFIE'S MOTHER
SOFIE'S FATHER
RAT CATCHER 1
RAT CATCHER 2
PIED PIPER
NARRATORS 1–4
RATS
CATS
SOUND EFFECTS

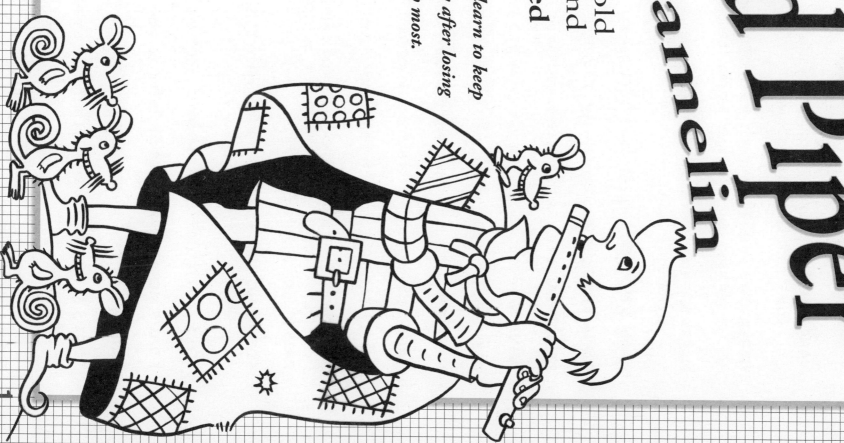

1

SCENE 1

NARRATOR 1 Long ago in Germany, there was a lovely little village called Hamelin (HAM luhn).

NARRATOR 2 Hamelin was surrounded by hills and mountains. A gentle river flowed near the edge of the town.

NARRATOR 3 When Hamelin's children filled the air with laughter, their parents thought Hamelin was the most beautiful place on earth.

NARRATOR 4 But the children didn't laugh often, because Hamelin had a problem. A big problem.

ANNA'S MOTHER Anna, why haven't you gotten dressed yet?

ANNA I can't get dressed. There are rats in my clothes!

ANNA'S FATHER Go away, you nasty rats! Go on! Shoo!

ANNA Make them go away! They're chewing up my brand new dress!

RATS Hiss! Growl! Squeak! Squeak!

HANS'S MOTHER Hans, why aren't you eating your lunch?

HANS I can't eat lunch. There are rats in my food.

HANS'S FATHER Go away, you nasty rats! Go on! Get out of here!

HANS Make them go away! They're drinking my milk and eating my bread!

RATS Squeal! Squeak! Growl! Hiss!

SOFIE'S MOTHER Sofie, why aren't you in bed? It's late. You should be sleeping.

SOFIE I can't go to bed. (*She whispers.*) There are rats under my covers.

SOFIE'S MOTHER Sofie, rats don't hide in people's beds. Here. I'll show you.

RATS Growl! Hiss! Squeal! Squeak!

SOFIE'S FATHER (*screams*) Eek! Go away, you nasty rats! This is a bed, not a rats' nest!

SOFIE Please make them go away! They've been gnawing on my toes!

NARRATOR 1 All the parents shooed the rats away with brooms.

RATS Squeak! Squeak! Hiss! Growl!

NARRATOR 2 But the rats came back.

ANNA'S FATHER These rats aren't afraid of anything. What are we to do?

SOFIE'S FATHER I have an idea. Let's offer a reward of . . . let's see, how much?

HANS'S MOTHER How about a thousand guilders (GIL derz)?

ANNA'S MOTHER That's a lot of cash!

HANS'S MOTHER I know. But think of the health and welfare of our children!

HANS'S FATHER If someone can get rid of these rats, that will be a small price to pay.

SOFIE'S FATHER All right, then. The reward will be a thousand guilders.

SCENE 2

NARRATOR 3 People came from all over Germany to try to earn the reward.

RAT CATCHER 1 I am the world's greatest inventor. I'm here to get rid of your rats. The reward is one thousand guilders. Is that correct?

HANS'S MOTHER Yes, a thousand guilders.

RAT CATCHER 1 Then behold! I have invented the world's most perfect rattrap.

ANNA The rats in Hamelin are pretty smart—maybe too smart for your traps.

RAT CATCHER 1 Nonsense, rats are stupid creatures. Just watch. I place the cheese here in the trap. Behold! The rats are sniffing the cheese. They will surely eat it.

ANNA Look! The clever rats have taken the cheese without setting off the traps!

ANNA'S FATHER No thousand guilders for you!

RAT CATCHER 1 Oh, rats!

SCENE 3

HANS Who are you?

RAT CATCHER 2 I am the world's greatest animal trainer. I'm here to get rid of your rats. The reward is a thousand guilders, right?

ANNA'S MOTHER Yes, a thousand guilders.

RAT CATCHER 2 Then feast your eyes on this! I've brought a hundred cats with me. They're the best rat hunters in the land. Your rats will be gone in no time.

CATS Meow! MEOW! Meow!

HANS The rats in Hamelin are pretty fierce. They may be too fierce for your cats.

RAT CATCHER 2 Nonsense. My ferocious cats will make mincemeat out of your puny rats. See those rats over there? All right cats, go get 'em!

RATS Growl! Hiss! Squeak! Squeal!

CATS MEOW! Meow! Hiss!

HANS Look! The cats are running away!

HANS'S FATHER No thousand guilders for you!

RAT CATCHER 2 Oh, rats!

SOPHIE'S MOTHER Will no one rid us of these rats?

SCENE 4

NARRATOR 4 Then one day another stranger appeared. He was the strangest looking man the town had ever seen.

NARRATOR 1 His eyes were bright. When he walked, he scampered like a bird.

NARRATOR 2 His long, lanky body looked as light as a feather.

NARRATOR 3 But the strangest thing about this stranger was the coat he wore. It was made of nothing but patches. Patches of many different colors.

SOFIE That man looks like a bird.

HANS Like a magpie!

ANNA We can call him the "pied" man because of all his patches.

HANS'S MOTHER Who are you?

NARRATOR 4 The man reached into his coat and pulled out a musical instrument.

SOFIE Oh, he's a piper. Then we shall call him the "pied piper."

PIED PIPER I'm here for the reward. It's a thousand guilders, right?

HANS'S FATHER Yes, a thousand guilders—but only if you get rid of the rats.

PIED PIPER I can rid you of the rats. Just promise me the thousand guilders.

ALL PARENTS We promise.

SOFIE How are you going to do it?

NARRATOR 1 The man just smiled. He put the pipe to his lips and began to blow.

SOUND EFFECTS *(like a flute)* Toot-a-toot-toot, Tat-a-tat-tat, Root-a-toot-toot.

NARRATOR 2 The rats at Sofie's house heard the Pied Piper's beautiful tune. They poured out of her bed and ran to the Pied Piper's feet.

NARRATOR 3 The rats in Hans's house heard the Pied Piper's tune. They dropped Hans's food and scurried to the Pied Piper's feet.

NARRATOR 4 The rats at Anna's house heard the Pied Piper's tune. They stopped chewing her clothes and scampered to the Pied Piper's feet.

NARRATOR 1 Soon all the rats in Hamelin were gathered at the Pied Piper's feet.

NARRATOR 2 The Pied Piper kept playing his tune.

SOUND EFFECTS Toot-a-toot-toot, Tat-a-tat-tat, Root-a-toot-toot.

NARRATOR 3 Slowly he walked toward the river.

NARRATOR 4 The rats followed behind him. They were practically dancing.

NARRATOR 1 The Pied Piper walked into the river.

NARRATOR 2 The rats followed him as if they were under a magic spell.

NARRATOR 3 The Pied Piper kept walking until he dipped beneath the water.

NARRATOR 4 One by one, the rats disappeared behind him.

SCENE 5

SOFIE Where is he? Where's the Pied Piper?

NARRATOR 1 Suddenly there was a splash.

NARRATOR 2 The Pied Piper walked out of the river.

NARRATOR 3 But no rats followed him this time. They had all drowned.

ANNA'S MOTHER He did it!

ANNA No more rats in my clothes!

HANS No more rats in my food!

SOFIE No more rats in my bed!

ANNA'S FATHER How can we ever thank you?

PIED PIPER Just give me the thousand guilders. That will be thanks enough.

NARRATOR 4 The parents stared at the Pied Piper.

NARRATOR 1 He looked ridiculous. He was all wet, his hair caked with mud.

SOFIE'S FATHER A thousand guilders is a lot of money.

PIED PIPER Yes, I know.

HANS'S MOTHER All you did was toot your pipe. That's not much work for a thousand gliders.

PIED PIPER I got rid of the rats.

ANNA'S MOTHER And now the rats are gone.

PIED PIPER So give me my thousand guilders.

HANS'S FATHER Why? We have better things to do with our hard-earned money!

PIED PIPER But you promised!

SOPHIE'S FATHER That, Sir, is your problem. I'm afraid there's nothing you can do about it!

NARRATOR 2 The Pied Piper shook his head sadly.

PIED PIPER Is "no" your final answer?

SOPHIE'S MOTHER Of course!

ANNA'S FATHER We say what we mean and mean what we say.

HANS'S MOTHER Everybody, let's go home.

SCENE 6

NARRATOR 3 The Pied Piper put the pipe to his lips and began to blow. Once again, the air was filled with beautiful musical tones.

SOUND EFFECTS Toot-a-toot-toot, Tat-a-tat-tat, Root-a-toot-toot.

NARRATOR 4 Anna listened to the Pied Piper's tune. She left her parents' side and skipped over to the Pied Piper.

NARRATOR 1 Hans listened to the Pied Piper's tune. He dropped his father's hand and jumped over to the Pied Piper.

The Pied Piper of Hamelin   7

NARRATOR 2 Sofie listened to the Pied Piper's tune. She pulled away from her mother's arms and ran over to the Pied Piper.

NARRATOR 3 Soon all the village children gathered around the Pied Piper.

NARRATOR 4 The Pied Piper kept playing his tune.

SOUND EFFECTS Toot-a-toot-toot, Tat-a-tat-tat, Root-a-toot-toot.

NARRATOR 1 Slowly he walked toward the mountains.

NARRATOR 2 The children followed behind him. They were practically dancing.

NARRATOR 3 The parents stood motionless as if under a magic spell.

NARRATOR 4 They tried to call out, but none of their mouths would move.

NARRATOR 1 They tried to run after the children but couldn't lift their feet.

NARRATOR 2 Suddenly a door opened up in the middle of the mountain. Slowly, the Piper walked through it.

NARRATOR 3 One by one, the children walked through the door behind him.

NARRATOR 4 And then, when the last child had passed through it, the door in the mountain closed . . . and disappeared.

NARRATOR 1 The parents of Hamelin searched for months and for years.

NARRATOR 2 But the door in the mountain never appeared again.

NARRATOR 3 And Hamelin never again echoed with the laughter of children.

NARRATOR 4 For the sake of a thousand guilders, the parents lost the most precious things in their lives.

Rescue the Pufflings!

by Don Abramson

The baby birds may be doomed unless the children can capture them—and then let them go!

CHARACTERS

LAURA BRIDGES (8 years)
KEITH BRIDGES (10 years)
MR. BRIDGES
MRS. BRIDGES
MAGGIE JONSON (12 years)
FRED JONSON (9 years)
MR. JONSON
MRS. JONSON
STOREKEEPER
HOTEL CLERK
GIRL 1
BOY 1
GIRL 2
BOY 2
NARRATORS 1–6

SCENE 1

NARRATOR 1 Laura and Keith Bridges are on a vacation.

NARRATOR 2 They are also on an adventure.

NARRATOR 3 It is early in August, and they have traveled with their mother and father to visit their cousins, Maggie and Fred Jonson, in Iceland.

NARRATOR 4 Iceland is a large island in the North Atlantic Ocean, between Greenland and Norway.

NARRATOR 5 So they had to take a plane to get there. But right now they are riding on a ferry boat, heading for another island, a place called Heimaey (HAY muh ay).

NARRATOR 6 All the cousins are leaning over the railing in front of the boat, watching the choppy ocean water pass below.

KEITH Maggie, how much longer until we get to this island?

MAGGIE The boat ride is supposed to take about two hours, so we'll be there pretty soon, Keith.

LAURA Is there a lot of fun stuff to do there?

MAGGIE Well, no, Laura. There's not a lot to do there at all. Heimaey is a pretty small island. And the town isn't very big.

FRED But you're going to have fun anyway—just wait and see.

KEITH How do you know, Fred?

FRED Because we're going to rescue pufflings. I bet you've never done anything like that back in [fill in your state].

KEITH We sure haven't.

LAURA What's a puffling? Mom and Dad told us about puffins, and showed us a picture——

MAGGIE A puffin is the adult bird, with all its black and white feathers.

FRED And its orange legs and feet, and its funny orange beak. That's why I like puffins!

MAGGIE But the baby chick is called a puffling.

KEITH But why do we have to rescue them?

MAGGIE Just a minute. There are your parents, with ours. *(Calling.)* Mom, Dad! We're over here!

MR. JONSON There you are. Hi, kids. Keith, Laura, are you enjoying your boat ride?

LAURA We sure are, Uncle Stefan. We've never been on a ferry boat before.

MRS. JONSON There's a plane that only takes about thirty minutes, but we thought this would be more fun.

LAURA It is, Aunt Helga, it is.

KEITH Mom, Dad, Maggie was just telling us about rescuing pufflings.

MRS. BRIDGES Good, then we can all hear it.

MR. BRIDGES It's the reason you told us we should come visit in August, isn't it?

MRS. JONSON Yes, it is, really. Go ahead, Maggie.

MAGGIE Well, when the little pufflings come out of their caves—

KEITH Wait a minute! Birds don't live in caves!

MAGGIE *(laughing)* You'd better tell him, Dad.

MR. JONSON Yes, they do, Keith. Actually, they live in burrows in the cliffs facing the sea. The puffins dig these burrows in the sides of the cliffs to lay their eggs in.

MRS. JONSON Then when the eggs hatch, the mother and father puffins take turns catching fish to feed their baby chicks.

MR. JONSON And so every year about this time, the pufflings are ready to leave their nests. They crawl out of their burrows at night, and they're supposed to fly right into the ocean, where they will live for the next couple of years.

FRED But that's when things go wrong, huh, Dad?

MRS. JONSON We don't know for sure whether some of the pufflings get confused by the lights of the town or what. But some of the babies start flying in the wrong direction. And then they find themselves on the streets and all over the town.

MR. JONSON And the trouble is, their wings aren't strong enough yet, so they can't take off from the ground.

MAGGIE So there they are, stuck.

FRED And it's dangerous, because there's all this traffic on the streets. They could get run over by a car or a truck.

MAGGIE Or worse—there are cats and dogs roaming around, and if they get hold of a puffling—

FRED It's goodbye, puffling!

LAURA Ewww! Gross!

KEITH So we have to rescue them?

MRS. BRIDGES That's right, Keith.

KEITH Then we'll be heroes, right, Dad?

MR. BRIDGES (laughing) I guess you will.

NARRATOR 1 Just then they hear a shout.

NARRATOR 2 (shouting) There they are, the puffins!

NARRATOR 3 Look, the puffins!

NARRATOR 4 And all of a sudden, the air is filled with birds—

NARRATOR 5 Puffins, gulls, and other sea birds—

ALL AVAILABLE VOICES (Ad lib caws, screeches, and other bird calls, so that the air is filled with noises.)

NARRATOR 6 Catching fish and carrying them away—

NARRATOR 1 Back to their nests, and their hungry chicks.

SCENE 2

NARRATOR 2 Later, on the island, the two families head for their hotel.

MR. JONSON Wait a minute, everyone. We need to stop in here for something.

MRS. BRIDGES This looks like a grocery store.

MR. JONSON It is.

MR. BRIDGES But I thought we were going to eat at our hotel.

MRS. JONSON Oh, we are. We're not here to buy food.

STOREKEEPER Good afternoon, folks. And what can I help you with today?

MRS. JONSON Maggie?

MAGGIE Hello. We would like some of your cardboard boxes, please.

STOREKEEPER Oh ho, here to rescue pufflings, are you?

MAGGIE Yes, we are.

STOREKEEPER Well, there's a stack of boxes over there against the wall. I've been saving them for weeks. You can take as many as you like.

MAGGIE Thank you.

STOREKEEPER You folks aren't from around here, are you?

KEITH No, we're not.

LAURA We're from [fill in your town and state]. How did you know?

STOREKEEPER Oh, I know just about everybody on this island. I think it's terrific, all you kids willing to rescue the poor baby birds. Sometimes people have got to help nature out a bit.

NARRATOR 3 Next, the families go to check into their hotel.

HOTEL CLERK Welcome to Heimaey, and here are your keys. Your rooms are on the second floor, right up those stairs.

MR. BRIDGES Thank you.

FRED I hope your hotel allows pets.

HOTEL CLERK (*laughing*) Why, yes we do, overnight pets. Just be sure you release them in the morning.

FRED Oh, we will!

MRS. BRIDGES I was wondering—what time do you think we should go out?

HOTEL CLERK Oh, ten o'clock, maybe. Things start getting pretty busy after that.

MR. BRIDGES Good. Well, kids, that gives us plenty of time to unpack, look at the town a bit, have dinner—

MRS. BRIDGES And maybe even catch a nap before we go out.

LAURA A nap! Mom, we don't need a nap!

KEITH We'll be much too excited to sleep!

SCENE 3

NARRATOR 4 However, later that night—

MR. BRIDGES Kids, wake up. Laura, Keith, it's ten o'clock.

MRS. BRIDGES Get dressed quickly. It's time to go out and be heroes.

MR. BRIDGES Here's a flashlight for each of you. And be sure to wear your gloves. These birds may be babies, but they still have sharp claws and a beak.

MRS. BRIDGES And don't forget your cardboard box.

NARRATOR 5 As the Bridges and Jonson families come out of their hotel, they see the streets are already filled with children running and hunting.

NARRATOR 6 The beams of their flashlights dance from trees to fences to houses.

NARRATOR 1 A couple of island children approach them, carrying their own cardboard box.

GIRL 1 Hello, you're visitors here, aren't you?

MAGGIE Yes, we are.

BOY 1 Well, good luck. We made a good start.

FRED Have you caught a puffling already? Can we see it?

GIRL 1 Sure, just shine your flashlight in the box here.

LAURA Oooh! It's cute!

KEITH That doesn't look like a puffin, though.

BOY 1 That's because it hasn't got its adult feathers yet. Give it a month or so.

LAURA It doesn't seem to mind being in your box.

MAGGIE There are still some pufflings out, aren't there?

GIRL 1 Maybe the box reminds it of its home nest. Well, we've got to go now.

BOY 1 Oh, there will be plenty. Just you wait.

BOY 2 (calling off) Look, there goes one!

GIRL 2 (calling off) Quick, chase it!

BOY 2 Where'd it go?

GIRL 2 It ran behind that mailbox, I think.

NARRATOR 2 And so Laura and Keith, Maggie and Fred start their own puffling hunt.

KEITH I see one—there—there it goes!

LAURA I didn't think they could run so fast!

KEITH Shine your flashlight over here—here, it's backed up against this fence.

LAURA Careful, don't hurt it!

KEITH I won't. Uh—there! Into the box you go, little guy!

LAURA Now I want to catch one.

NARRATOR 3 And so into the night, children run up one street and down another, searching through alleys, behind shops, underneath parked cars.

GIRL 2 There goes another one!

BOY 2 I see it. Quick!

GIRL 1 I've got another one!

BOY 1 Over here, your flashlight.

NARRATOR 4 Laura and Keith end up with four pufflings. The little birds spend the night—"overnight pets"—in the cardboard box in the bathtub.

SCENE 4

NARRATOR 5 The next morning, the two families set out on the second part of their adventure—releasing the pufflings they have caught.

KEITH I'll bet when these little birds crawled out of their burrows last night, they never expected to be riding in a cardboard box on a bus.

MAGGIE Well, we've got to take them to the other side of the island to release them.

LAURA But there's a harbor right in town. Why can't they just go swimming there?

MR. JONSON But Laura, did you notice the water in that harbor?

MRS. JONSON This is a fishing town, and there's a lot of boat traffic in and out of that harbor, in addition to the ferries and shipping. It leaves the water polluted with oil and other gunk.

MAGGIE I know, if they got that oil on their feathers, they could die.

MR. JONSON But here we are at the lighthouse. Now we'll climb down the hill to the edge of the cliff.

MRS. BRIDGES Careful—don't go too near the edge.

LAURA What do we do now?

MR. BRIDGES Well, here are some other kids, releasing their catches from last night.

GIRL 2 Hello, is this your first time?

LAURA Yes, it is.

KEITH How do you let the pufflings go? I guess you don't just dump them out of the boxes.

GIRL 2 Oh, no. Hold the puffling in both hands, like this. Loosely, so it can flap its wings. And then you swing it down and up, down and up, down and then throw it up as high as you can over the water. And I always say, "Fly away!"

KEITH Here, let me try. One, two—Fly away!

LAURA Look at it go! (*Laughs.*) It's flapping its wings as hard as it can!

FRED Huh, it didn't fly very far, did it? Only just plunked down in the water.

MAGGIE But at least it's in the ocean, where it's supposed to be. And now it can fish and take care of itself.

LAURA My turn, now.

KEITH Here's the box—

LAURA Don't be scared, little puffling. I won't hurt you. You're going to fly now. You're going home. One, two—fly away!

ALL AVAILABLE VOICES *(ad lib, so the effect is that of dozens of children all over the island releasing their birds)* Fly away!

KEITH Mom, Dad, you know what? This is the best vacation ever!

LAURA You know what I like? First it's fun to catch the pufflings, to run around at night and put them in boxes and all. But you know what's even better? To let them go!

ALL AVAILABLE VOICES *(whispering ad lib)* Fly away! Fly away! Fly away!

Alice Drives into History

by Amy Fellner Dominy

In 1909, no woman had ever driven across America. Could Alice Ramsey be the first?

CHARACTERS

ALICE RAMSEY
HERMINE JAHNS
MARGARET ATWOOD
NETTIE POWELL
JOHN MURPHY
OHIO WOMAN
NARRATORS 1–5
CRITICS 1–3
TOWNSPEOPLE 1–2

SCENE 1

NARRATOR 1 In 1909, Alice Ramsey wanted to be the first woman to drive a car across America.

NARRATOR 2 In those days, not many people had cars, and there were few paved roads. Traveling by car outside of cities and towns was rough— even dangerous. There were very few car repair shops. If your car broke down, you could get stuck anywhere.

NARRATOR 3 Alice Ramsey had a lot of critics. They were people who criticized her plans and made fun of her.

CRITIC 1 Drive across America? Are you crazy, Alice? No woman can do that.

ALICE Maybe, but I'm still going to do it.

CRITIC 2 It'll take months over terrible roads.

CRITIC 3 You'll have to climb mountains, cross rivers, and drive across deserts.

ALICE Then that's what I'll do.

CRITIC 1 You'll never make it alone.

HERMINE I'll go with her. I'm her friend, Hermine.

MARGARET I'll go too. I'm her sister-in-law, Margaret. How about you, Nettie?

NETTIE Well, I'm her sister-in-law too. If you're going, Margaret, I'm going.

CRITIC 2 You're all crazy.

JOHN Then I must be crazy too. I'm John Murphy, a reporter for the Boston *Herald*. I'll travel ahead of your car, Alice, and give you a hand when you need help. And by the way, please call me John.

NARRATOR 4 July 9, 1909, was a rainy day in New York City. In spite of the weather, crowds gathered to watch Alice and her companions start their long journey.

CRITIC 3 Are you sure you won't give up this crazy scheme, Alice?

ALICE Never!

CRITIC 1 Just wait. You'll quit soon enough.

NARRATOR 5 Alice didn't listen. She strode through the muddy puddles to the front of the car.

NARRATOR 1 She gave the crank a mighty spin.

NARRATOR 2 The engine of her Maxwell Motor Car roared to life.

ALICE California, here we come!

SCENE 2

NARRATOR 3 They were off. But Alice had to do more than just drive. She had to take care of the car.

NARRATOR 4 She used a stick to measure their gasoline. At night, she lit the gas headlamps with a match!

NARRATOR 5 If the car broke down, Alice had to fix it. She also had to figure out which way to go.

NARRATOR 1 Alice drove her companions through New York and Pennsylvania.

NARRATOR 2 Then they started into Ohio, where they soon got lost.

MARGARET We've been driving up and down this road for hours.

HERMINE The only directions for motorists are in this Blue Book. It doesn't have pictures. It only says to find the yellow barn and turn right.

MARGARET There is no yellow barn on this road.

NETTIE Then how to do we decide where to turn?

MARGARET Let's ask that woman up ahead.

ALICE Excuse me, Ma'am. We're looking for a yellow barn.

OHIO WOMAN Oh, it's right back there.

HERMINE But that barn is green.

OHIO WOMAN It is now. It used to be yellow. The man who lives there hates cars. He painted the barn green just to confuse all the motorists.

HERMINE I think we need a better map.

ALICE There isn't one. And once we get west of the Missouri River, there are no maps at all!

NARRATOR 3 From there, Alice and her friends traveled through Indiana and Illinois.

NARRATOR 4 As they moved west, the roads got so bad, they began driving to a new rhythm.

ALICE Lurch.

HERMINE Jerk.

MARGARET Skid.

NETTIE Bounce.

ALICE Lurch.

HERMINE Jerk.

MARGARET Skid.

NETTIE CRASH!

NARRATOR 5 The car got stuck in ruts and prairie dog holes. Once, a horse and cart had to pull them out.

NARRATOR 1 The brake pedal broke. The axle snapped.

NARRATOR 2 Tires exploded—eleven different times!

NARRATOR 3 They got soaked by rain, pelted by hail, and splattered with mud.

SCENE 3

NARRATOR 4 At Weasel Creek, Iowa, the trip came to a stop.

HERMINE Oh no! Just look at this creek!

MARGARET It must be flooded from all the rain.

ALICE I'll wade across and see how deep it is.

NETTIE Be careful, Alice. Go slowly.

ALICE The water is cold on my ankles. I'll just take a few more steps and—AH!

HERMINE, MARGARET, and NETTIE Alice!

ALICE I'm okay. The water just got very deep. It's all the way up to my waist. We can't drive the car through this.

MARGARET We'll have to turn back.

ALICE No, we won't. We can wait it out.

HERMINE I'll see if I can buy us some dinner at the farmhouse we passed.

NETTIE With no food or shelter?

ALICE Good idea, Hermine.

NARRATOR 5 Soon, Hermine returned.

HERMINE I got us a loaf of bread, butter, and a jar of water—all for twenty-five cents!

ALICE And tonight, we'll put our feet on the dashboard and sleep in the car.

NARRATOR 1 After a miserable night, they woke up to find the creek was down.

NARRATOR 2 Alice's patience had paid off.

ALICE We're back in business, ladies.

ALICE, HERMINE, MARGARET, and NETTIE On to Boone, Iowa!

NARRATOR 3 And more muddy problems!

NARRATOR 4 People from the town warned Alice.

TOWNSPERSON 1 Up ahead is Danger Hill. It's so steep, most cars slide right down.

TOWNSPERSON 2 You'll never make it up. Your load is too heavy!

TOWNSPERSON 1 You'll have to put your car on the train and ship it to Nebraska.

ALICE I promised to drive every inch of this trip, and that's what I'm going to do!

TOWNSPERSON 2 That's what you say now. You haven't seen Danger Hill.

NETTIE Well, you haven't seen us ladies in action, Gentlemen. This is what we'll do. Margaret, Hermine, and I will take our bags and go to Nebraska by train.

HERMINE Great idea, Nettie. Then Alice can drive up the hill with a lighter car.

JOHN I'll go with you, Alice, so you won't be alone.

ALICE I'll be glad for the company, John.

JOHN I'll write a story for the newspaper along the way.

NARRATOR 5 Alice and John started the journey the next morning.

NARRATOR 1 The car slipped and skidded on the muddy roads, but Alice never lost control.

NARRATOR 2 She made it up Danger Hill safely.

JOHN I'm going to write a great newspaper story about this, Alice.

ALICE Thanks, John. Now, I'd better drive on to Nebraska and rejoin my friends.

SCENE 4

NARRATOR 3 Together again, Alice drove her companions into the rugged state of Wyoming.

HERMINE What kind of squatty, flat-topped hills are those, Alice?

ALICE They're called buttes.

MARGARET And these hills seem to be huge piles of loose rock and gravel.

NETTIE Will the car make it up?

ALICE Let's give it a try.

NARRATOR 4 Slowly, the Maxwell climbed up the hill.

NARRATOR 5 Then slid back down.

NARRATOR 1 Again they climbed up.

NARRATOR 2 And slid back down.

HERMINE What can we do, Alice?

ALICE I have an idea. The three of you walk beside the car. When it begins to slide down, set a piece of wood behind the tires to stop us. Then, I'll start up again and we'll inch our way up this hill.

NARRATOR 3 Slowly but surely, they made it over the hills of Wyoming and into the state of Utah.

NARRATOR 4 They hoped the worst was behind them.

NARRATOR 5 Or was it just up ahead?

CRITIC 2 I can't believe Alice has made it this far!

CRITIC 3 Well, now she's coming up to hot, dusty desert—miles and miles of it.

CRITIC 1 She'll turn back for sure.

SCENE 5

NARRATOR 1 On July 31, Alice and her friends reached the Nevada desert.

HERMINE Not much to see but tumbleweeds.

MARGARET And those prickly horned-toads.

NETTIE And—wait! What's that in the distance?

MARGARET There's a big dust cloud. And it's coming this way.

NETTIE It's getting closer. It's—

ALICE, HERMINE, NETTIE, and MARGARET Indians!

ALICE Stay calm, everyone.

HERMINE Calm? With a dozen Indians galloping toward us?

NETTIE They've got bows and arrows!

HERMINE I'm closing my eyes!

MARGARET Me, too!

NETTIE Me, three!

ALICE Well, would you look at that!

HERMINE, MARGARET, and NETTIE We can't look. Our eyes are closed!

ALICE It's just a hunting party. The Indians are hunting that jackrabbit. Look at it go!

HERMINE Even better, look at the Indians go after it.

MARGARET That jackrabbit isn't racing as fast as my heart. Let's get out of here!

NARRATOR 2 Alice drove them safely through the Nevada desert.

ALICE The last big hurdle is up ahead—the Sierra Nevada Mountains.

CRITIC 2 Alice will never make it up the mountains.

CRITIC 3 It's eighty-one miles straight up into the clouds.

CRITIC 1 She'll have to quit for sure.

NARRATOR 3 On August third, Alice gripped the steering wheel tight, and began to climb the Sierra Nevadas.

NARRATOR 4 The car struggled up the steep, sandy road.

NARRATOR 5 The engine got dangerously hot.

NARRATOR 1 Alice stopped at each hairpin turn to cool the engine.

ALICE And while we're here, we might as well admire the view.

HERMINE Those blue skies seem endless, don't they?

MARGARET And those peaks in the distance—blues and purples and all hazy. It's so beautiful here!

ALICE Guess what, ladies. We're going to put up in style tonight. The Maxwell car people have paid for a night for us at a cottage at Lakeside Park.

NETTIE Good. We can do a few repairs on our clothes.

MARGARET We want to look good for the big finale.

HERMINE Oh, no! My best straw hat—it got crushed in the suitcase!

NETTIE I've got some silk chiffon I can stitch across the crown to hide the damage.

HERMINE Thank you, Nettie.

NARRATOR 2 Finally, Alice made it over the last summit.

ALICE Here we are, ladies—California!

SCENE 6

NARRATOR 3 Once they had come through the high mountains, it was an easy ride to the end of the road—San Francisco.

HERMINE You did it, Alice!

MARGARET The first woman to drive a car across the United States!

NETTIE Who knows, Alice. Maybe someday, people will write stories about you!

NARRATOR 4 On August 7, 1909, Alice and her companions arrived in San Francisco.

NARRATOR 5 A parade of cars followed Alice's Maxwell through the city.

ALL VOICES (ad lib) Yay, Alice! You did it! Honk! Honk!

CRITIC 2 I can't believe she did it.

CRITIC 3 Yeah, but I'll bet she was slow.

NARRATOR 1 Alice completed the journey in fifty-nine days—faster than any man had done it before.

ALL CRITICS (ad lib) Well . . . uh . . . .

NARRATOR 2 Alice silenced all the critics who believed she couldn't do it.

NARRATOR 3 Because Alice believed in herself. She was one of a kind!

CHARACTERS

LITTLE CIGUAPA
FELIPE (8 years)
LAURA (9 years)
MAMÁ CIGUAPA
PAPÁ CIGUAPA
DEER
FROG
FALCON
MOUSE
LIZARD
AUNT ZELDA
VILLAGERS 1–2
NARRATORS 1–5

STRANGE CREATURES

based on a legend from the Dominican Republic

by Laurel Haines

*When Laura and Felipe get lost in the forest,
Little Ciguapa rescues them. But soon they
find they must rescue her in return!*

SCENE 1

NARRATOR 1 Deep in the forest on the island of the Dominican Republic, there once lived a magical creature.

NARRATOR 2 Her name was Little Ciguapa (see GWAH pah), and though she looked human, she was not.

NARRATOR 3 She had long hair that reached down to her toes.

NARRATOR 4 She could talk to animals.

NARRATOR 5 But what made Little Ciguapa most different from other creatures was this: her feet were on backwards.

NARRATOR 1 But she did not know this. She thought that everyone's toes pointed backwards . . .

NARRATOR 2 And heels faced forwards.

NARRATOR 3 When she ran through the forest, her footprints ran the other way.

NARRATOR 4 One morning Little Ciguapa was sleeping in her tree when she heard a familiar voice calling. It was her best friend, Deer.

DEER Little Ciguapa! Wake up! Wake up!

LITTLE CIGUAPA What's going on, Deer?

DEER The guanabana (gwah NAH bah nah) fruit are ripening.

LITTLE CIGUAPA Oh, I love guanabana fruit. Let's get some!

NARRATOR 5 Little Ciguapa jumped out of her tree and ran with Deer to the guanabana trees. Soon, other animal friends came to share the tasty fruit.

FROG Ribbitt! Ribbitt! Achoo! Achoo!

LITTLE CIGUAPA Hello, Froggy. How are you today?

FROG I've got a bad cold that won't go away.

LITTLE CIGUAPA Then eat this fruit. We use it to cure all sorts of ills.

NARRATOR 1 Suddenly Little Ciguapa heard a strange noise. Now, all the animals in the forest had good hearing, but Little Ciguapa's ears were the best of all.

NARRATOR 2 She could even hear fish blowing bubbles in nearby streams.

NARRATOR 3 But this sound was unlike any other.

FELIPE Laura, come here! You'll get lost.

LAURA We're already lost, Felipe. How can I get more lost?

FELIPE Stay close to me. Why, oh why did we wander this far?

LAURA Because I wanted to see the Ciguapa!

FELIPE Silly! There's no such thing as a Ciguapa. It's a made-up story.

NARRATOR 4 Little Ciguapa scrambled to the top of a tall tree to get a better look.

LITTLE CIGUAPA Deer and Froggy, where are those noises coming from?

FROG What do you see up there, Little Ciguapa?

LITTLE CIGUAPA I see two strange creatures, Froggy. They look something like me, except their hair is short, and their feet . . .

DEER What about their feet?

LITTLE CIGUAPA Their feet are on backwards, Deer! If only I could see them better!

FALCON Screech! Screech!

NARRATOR 5 Just then a falcon flew nearby.

LITTLE CIGUAPA Falcon! Fly over there and tell me what you see.

NARRATOR 1 The Falcon did as Little Ciguapa asked and soon returned.

FALCON Little Ciguapa, there are human children over there—two of them.

LITTLE CIGUAPA I've never seen humans, but Momma said to keep clear of them.

FALCON Good advice. But since these are children, Little Ciguapa, I think we don't need to fear them.

SCENE 2

FELIPE I don't see another soul around here, Laura.

LAURA Just that falcon up there, Felipe. I wish we could ask him where we are.

FELIPE Laura, look! I see footprints!

LAURA Yes, like someone was walking barefoot here.

FELIPE They're fresh. This person must be nearby. Let's follow the footprints!

LAURA Wait a minute, Felipe. What if this person is unfriendly?

FELIPE The footprints are small, Laura. I bet this is a kid, like us. Come on!

LAURA You're right, Felipe. Let's go.

FALCON Look, Little Ciguapa, the human children are following your footprints.

LITTLE CIGUAPA But they're going backwards, Falcon, toward my tree!

DEER Let's follow them, Little Ciguapa.

LITTLE CIGUAPA Yes, Deer, let's.

NARRATOR 2 Little Ciguapa and the other animals followed the children through the forest, until they came to Little Ciguapa's tree.

FELIPE Laura, look! The footprints end at this tree.

LAURA Whoever it was must have climbed up the branches, Felipe. But I can't see anything through the leaves. Hello?

FELIPE Hello! Is anyone up there?

LITTLE CIGUAPA Just my parents. But don't wake them, they're still sleeping.

NARRATOR 3 Laura and Felipe turned around and saw Little Ciguapa.

LAURA It's a Ciguapa! You're real!

LITTLE CIGUAPA Of course I'm real. And I'm called Little Ciguapa.

LAURA Look at her, Felipe! Her feet are on backwards!

FELIPE Why, you're right, Laura. Her toes are pointing the wrong way!

LITTLE CIGUAPA Excuse me, but my feet are exactly right. Yours are on backwards.

FELIPE No, our feet are on forwards.

LITTLE CIGUAPA Backwards!

LAURA What's forwards to you, Little Ciguapa, is backwards to us humans.

MAMÁ CIGUAPA Who do I hear arguing down there, my Little Ciguapa?

LITTLE CIGUAPA Mamá! Papá! Look! I met humans!

PAPÁ CIGUAPA Little Ciguapa, stay away from them! They can hurt you!

LITTLE CIGUAPA They won't hurt me. They're lost.

FELIPE Please help us, Little Ciguapa. We need to find our way home.

LITTLE CIGUAPA Please Mamá, Papá! Let me help them find their way home.

MAMÁ CIGUAPA All right, little one. They look as though they need help. But stay away from all adult humans—and come home before nightfall.

PAPÁ CIGUAPA Falcon, you go with my child and the others. Make sure they stay safe.

FALCON I'll fly overhead and lead the way. I know the village where these children live. Screech! Screech!

FELIPE What is that falcon squawking about, Little Ciguapa?

LITTLE CIGUAPA Can't you humans understand him? He says he'll lead the way.

FELIPE Can you talk to animals, then?

LITTLE CIGUAPA Yes, can't you?

FELIPE No. How do you do it, Little Ciguapa?

LITTLE CIGUAPA Come on. I'll teach you while we walk back to your village.

SCENE 3

NARRATOR 4 So the Falcon, Little Ciguapa, Laura, and Felipe headed through the forest toward the children's village.

NARRATOR 5 Little Ciguapa tried to teach Laura and Felipe how to talk to animals.

LAURA Hello, Mouse. Hello, Lizard. How are you?

MOUSE Squeak! Squeak! I can't understand a word this human is saying.

LIZARD Hiss! Hiss! Little Ciguapa, what is she saying?

LITTLE CIGUAPA She's just saying hello, Lizard.

MOUSE Squeak! Sounds like gibberish to me.

LIZARD Hiss! Can't she speak in lizard language?

FELIPE Maybe we humans aren't meant to talk to animals, Laura.

LAURA Look, Felipe! I see the houses of our village now.

FELIPE And there's Aunt Zelda!

LAURA Aunt Zelda! It's us, Felipe and Laura!

AUNT ZELDA Children, we've been worried about you! Who is that with you?

LAURA We met Little Ciguapa!

AUNT ZELDA A Ciguapa! Everyone! Come look!

NARRATOR 1 Villagers came out of their houses to get a look at the Ciguapa.

VILLAGERS (*ad lib*) Let's catch her! Let's keep her as a pet!

LITTLE CIGUAPA Uh-oh! My parents were right to warn me. I'd better run fast!

NARRATOR 2 Little Ciguapa had never been in a village before.

NARRATOR 3 She tried to run away but couldn't find her way out.

NARRATOR 4 The streets and buildings were like a puzzle to her.

VILLAGER 1 There's the creature! Throw the net over her.

VILLAGER 2 Aha! Got her! Into the cage you go!

LAURA No! No! You must let Little Ciguapa go! She belongs in the forest.

VILLAGER 1 She won't escape now. I've locked the door tight.

VILLAGER 2 Why should we listen to you children? What's done is done.

VILLAGER 1 You know, I'll bet someone would be willing to pay a lot of money for a creature like that!

SCENE 4

NARRATOR 5 That night, trembling in fear, Little Ciguapa called to her friends.

LITTLE CIGUAPA Falcon! Froggy! Deer! Help me!

NARRATOR 1 The animals gathered around Little Ciguapa but could do nothing.

FALCON Screech! We can't open the door of your cage, Little Ciguapa. It's locked.

NARRATOR 2 Just then Little Ciguapa heard a door open in a house on the other side of the village, followed by footsteps. Those footsteps got louder and louder.

NARRATOR 3 Until at last Felipe and Laura appeared, completely out of breath.

FELIPE Little Ciguapa, we have the key!

NARRATOR 4 Without further delay, Felipe and Laura opened the door and let Little Ciguapa out of the cage. The animals danced with joy.

LITTLE CIGUAPA You saved me, my human friends!

LAURA Little Ciguapa, I'm sorry for what the villagers did to you. They just don't understand.

FELIPE Now run, Little Ciguapa, run! You have to get out of here.

LITTLE CIGUAPA But you are my friends now. When will I see you again?

LAURA I don't know. Felipe and I may not be able to visit you again.

FROG Ribbett! Little Ciguapa, you'll risk your life if you try to see these children again.

DEER It's too dangerous for us forest creatures to mix with humans.

LITTLE CIGUAPA Children, my forest friends advise me against seeing you again—and I must agree with them. But I shall never forget you. And thanks ever so much for setting me free!

FELIPE We'll never forget YOU, Little Ciguapa. Thanks for helping us get home.

LAURA Now go quickly, Little Ciguapa! I hear others coming!

LITTLE CIGUAPA Good-by!

NARRATOR 5 Little Ciguapa ran through the forest. And by the time the other humans found the empty cage, Little Ciguapa was back home in her tree.

NARRATOR 1 With her mother and father and all the other forest creatures.

What Does Freedom Mean?

by Alisha Fran-Potter

with students at Hoffman School, Glenview, Illinois

Freedom is a hard word to define,
but it means something quite real
to most people.

CHARACTERS

at the Pleasant River School
MICHAEL (9 years)
KEVIN (9 years)
MRS. RUTH KEATS (Gram)
MRS. TANE
MRS. WILDER
MARY (10 years)
AMY (9 years)
TESS (12 years)
YOUNG RUTH (12 years)
ANNA (11 years)

at the Senior Center
MR. SANCHEZ
MRS. THOMAS
MR. JOHN GARBASKI
YOUNG JOHN (9 years)
MOTHER GARBASKI
FATHER GARBASKI
MR. HENRY
CHRIS (16 years)

SCENE 1

MICHAEL Come on, Kevin—let's go to the playground.

KEVIN Michael, I can't play now. I have to do this project!

MICHAEL Well, it might not be so bad, Kevin. It might even be interesting.

KEVIN Yeah, interviewing a bunch of old people.

MICHAEL They all don't have to be old. Here, read the assignment Mrs. Karel handed out.

KEVIN "Write a report about what Freedom means. Interview three people. Two must be over 55, and the other can be any age. . . ." Gee, Michael, how do you know where to start?

MICHAEL Well, I'm gonna start with my grandma. I'm going over to her house at four o'clock. Do you want to come along? It might give you some ideas.

KEVIN Sounds good. Thanks.

SCENE 2

MICHAEL Hi! Gram, this is my friend Kevin.

KEVIN Hi, Mrs. Keats.

MRS. RUTH KEATS Well, hello, Kevin. Come in, both of you.

MICHAEL Gram, we have to do a report for school. Can we interview you?

MRS. RUTH KEATS Sure, what do you want to interview me about?

MICHAEL Well, the title of our report is "What Does Freedom Mean to You?"

MRS. RUTH KEATS I can tell you a lot about that!

MICHAEL Let's get our notebooks and pencils out, Kevin.

KEVIN Okay . . . ready, Mrs. Keats!

MRS. RUTH KEATS Well, boys, I was twelve when my parents died. I had to go live at a children's home called Pleasant River. It was anything but pleasant, I'll tell you! The headmistress was named Mrs. Tane, and . . .

SCENE 3

MRS. TANE Ruth, this is your room. You'll be sharing with Mary, Tess, and Amy.

YOUNG RUTH Thank you, Mrs. Tane.

MARY Hi, Ruth. I'm Mary.

AMY And I'm Amy.

TESS I'm Tess. Glad to meet you, Ruth.

YOUNG RUTH Hello Mary, Tess, and . . . Amy.

MRS. TANE Why don't you get settled, Ruth, and get to know the girls?

YOUNG RUTH Sure, Mrs. Tane. Thanks.

MARY So how come you ended up at Pleasant River, Ruth?

YOUNG RUTH Well, Mary, my parents died, and there isn't anyone to take care of me.

AMY Hard break.

YOUNG RUTH Yeah. Thanks, Amy.

MARY Look, a few pointers. Don't get into trouble with Mrs. Tane.

AMY Yeah, she doesn't give second chances.

TESS She's always getting mad at you about something or other.

MARY Another thing, Ruth—you can't leave without a pass.

YOUNG RUTH A pass, Mary?

TESS Yeah, a piece of paper. You know—to go to the store or the library.

MARY If you forget your pass, Ruth, you'll be in big trouble.

SCENE 4

MRS. WILDER Now class, today we will be taking a job survey.

TESS Excuse me, Mrs. Wilder. This is a new girl, Ruth.

MRS. WILDER Thank you, Tess. . . . Welcome to my class, Ruth. You may take the desk at the back of the room. There . . . good. Now back to our job survey.

ANNA What's a job survey?

MRS. WILDER It's a series of questions you answer. How you answer will tell us what kind of job you would do best.

ANNA I want to be a singer, Mrs. Wilder.

MRS. WILDER No, Anna. This test will tell us if you should be a secretary, a nurse, a teacher, a nanny, or a maid.

ANNA But why only those jobs, Mrs. Wilder?

MRS. WILDER Those are proper jobs for women, Anna. Ruth, you'll need to take the survey too, so we know what classes to put you in.

YOUNG RUTH I have my grades from my old school, Mrs. Wilder.

MRS. WILDER That doesn't matter, Ruth. The test will tell us where you belong.

YOUNG RUTH But—

MRS. WILDER No buts. We decide what classes you'll take for job training.

SCENE 5

MRS. RUTH KEATS That's what it was like at Pleasant River.

MICHAEL I didn't know you went to a school like that, Gram.

MRS. RUTH KEATS Oh, yes. I had no say in the classes I took or in much of anything else.

KEVIN Wow! That stinks!

MRS. RUTH KEATS Yes, it did, Kevin, but I had no choice, no freedoms. I wanted to be a nurse, but the test showed I would be best as a secretary.

KEVIN I don't think it's like that today, is it?

MRS. RUTH KEATS No, it's not. Young people—girls and boys—have many choices.

KEVIN My Grandma told me she tried to get a summer job in construction—you know, building things. But she was told, "girls can't do this work." Grandma was so mad, she went home and built a storage shed behind their house that day!

MRS. RUTH KEATS Why don't you interview her, Kevin?

KEVIN I'd like to. But she lives a long way from here.

MRS. RUTH KEATS You could call her on the phone. Ask your folks for permission—I'm sure they'd go along with the idea, Kevin.

KEVIN Great idea. Thanks!

MRS. RUTH KEATS I've got another idea, boys. I'm going to a meeting at the Senior Center. Why don't you come along and interview some people there?

KEVIN Sounds good. This might not be so bad after all!

SCENE 6

MRS. RUTH KEATS Well, here we are. This is the Senior Center, boys. Hello everybody. This is my grandson, Michael, and his friend, Kevin. They're working on a school project. They need to interview some of you, if you don't mind.

MR. SANCHEZ Sure, we like to talk.

MRS. RUTH KEATS Great! Kids, I'll be in Room 10 for my meeting if you need me.

KEVIN AND MICHAEL (ad lib) Okay. 'Bye. Thanks, Gram.

MR. SANCHEZ Hello, boys. I'm Mr. Sanchez. And this is Mrs. Thomas.

MRS. THOMAS Glad to meet you, boys.

MR. JOHN GARBASKI Hi. I'm John Garbaski. Just what is your school project about?

KEVIN Mr. Garbaski, we're supposed to ask people what freedom means to them.

MR. JOHN GARBASKI Fine! I'd like to tell you about why I came to America. It has to do with freedom.

KEVIN and MICHAEL That would be great, Mr. Garbaski!

MR. JOHN GARBASKI I was about your age, Kevin and Michael, when my family came here from Poland. My mother, my father, and me. It seems like yesterday. . . .

YOUNG JOHN I can't believe we made it to America, Mom and Dad!

MOTHER GARBASKI Yes, John. Now maybe we can earn a living . . .

FATHER GARBASKI And not go hungry like we did back home.

YOUNG JOHN Mom and Dad, I'm going to get a job to help you out.

FATHER GARBASKI Thanks John, but you need to go to school. Your mother and I will find jobs, and we'll be okay.

YOUNG JOHN But I can work now!

MOTHER GARBASKI Finish school and then work, son. You'll be able to get a much better job.

MR. JOHN GARBASKI Well, that's just what I did—I finished school.

KEVIN Then what?

MR. JOHN GARBASKI I got a job as a drugstore clerk. I worked hard—and finally became vice president of the company. That's not bad for a boy who couldn't speak English when he got here! . . . Mr. Henry? Do you have a story to tell?

MR. HENRY Yes, Mr. Garbaski. Kids, my granddaughter got married a few years ago. She and her husband couldn't have children, so they decided to adopt.

MICHAEL And . . . ?

MR. HENRY They have a wonderful son named Phillip who's three years old. But they wanted more. So they went outside the U. S. to adopt a little girl. They came back with twin girls! Now they have a fine, big family!

KEVIN That's cool! Freedom means being able to create a family if you want one!

SCENE 7

MICHAEL Mrs. Thomas, how about you?

MRS. THOMAS My freedom story takes place over time. It has to do with men and women in my family who've served in the army. My grandfather was in World War I, my father in World War II, my husband in Korea, my son in Vietnam, and now my granddaughter is in the army.

KEVIN But what does that have to do with freedom, Mrs. Thomas?

MRS. THOMAS Well, Kevin, our country has to be ready to defend freedom at a moment's notice. You know, kids, freedom is a gift, not a privilege. Sometimes we have to take a stand for freedom, even when it's not easy. Some people defend freedom on battlefields. Others do it by standing up for their beliefs in their schools and workplaces and by voting in elections.

MR. SANCHEZ Hi, Chris. Ready to set up our Bingo game?

CHRIS Sure, Mr. Sanchez.

MR. SANCHEZ Kids, this is Chris—he volunteers here at the center. Chris, meet Michael and Kevin. They're working on a school project. Kevin, is there a question you'd like to ask Chris?

KEVIN Yes. Hi, Chris. We're trying to find out what freedom means to different people. Would you tell us what freedom means to you?

CHRIS Sure, Kevin. My family came to America ten years ago, mainly for religious freedom. You see, the government was against our religion, so we had to worship in secret. Here we're free to worship as we please. That's freedom!

MR. SANCHEZ That's why the Pilgrims came to America, Chris. You're a pilgrim!

MICHAEL All your stories are cool. And they're all different. I think we have plenty of information now, Kevin.

KEVIN Right, Michael. I think we'd better get started writing our reports.

MR. HENRY When you finish, Michael and Kevin, we'd love to read them.

MICHAEL Sure, Mr. Henry. We'll come back next week and share our reports with all of you. We'd better go now. Mr. Garbaski, could you tell my Grandma we went home?

MR. GARBASKI Be happy to.

KEVIN AND MICHAEL 'Bye, everyone!

ALL AVAILABLE VOICES *(ad lib)* Good-by!

Poetry Interpretation

To **interpret** poetry means to read it aloud for an audience. You use your *voice*, your *body*, and your *facial expressions* to get the meaning of the poetry across.

Some poems tell stories. They name characters and describe the actions of the characters as they go to school, get in trouble, go on adventures, and so on. With poems like these, you need to figure out who the characters are. Characters may be people, animals, or even inanimate objects, like rocks or tools. You also need to figure out what the relationship is between the characters. Is there a conflict? That's important to understand.

Some storytelling poems have speeches, like dialogue in a play. A poem with dialogue may be just one long speech by one character. Then you can act that character's part when you interpret the poem.

A poem with dialogue may have speeches by two or more characters talking back and forth. Then you can read it with some friends, each of you acting one character's part. Or, you can act all the characters yourself. You can use different character voices and different facial expressions.

Other poems do not tell stories. They may simply describe interesting scenes or tell about how the speaker feels. Sometimes a reader can't be sure who the speaker is supposed to be. Then you might imagine yourself as the speaker. Imagine yourself feeling the way the speaker feels and using words the speaker uses.

WHAT DOES IT MEAN?

When you interpret poetry, your first job is to make the audience understand what is going on. To do that, you have to be sure you understand it yourself. Here are some pointers:

- *Understand every word.* Use a dictionary for any word you're not sure of. Remember that many words have more than one meaning. Also be sure you understand any references to fairy tales, myths, history, and so on.

- *Think about the title.* What does it tell you about the poem? Does it suggest new meanings for the poem?

- *Look for the meaning.* Look for complete sentences. Use punctuation to help you know when to pause. Some poems are not written in sentences. In that case, look for complete thoughts. Think about how you can use your voice to get those thoughts across.

WHAT SHOULD IT SOUND LIKE?

After you understand the poem, you have to get your understanding across to your audience. Ask yourself these questions:

- *What is the style or mood of the poem?* Is it funny or serious? Is it full of surprise or full of anger? Is it written in simple, everyday language or in more formal language?

- *What is the rhythm of the poem?* Does it call for a quick, light reading or a slow, thoughtful one? Be sure you stress the syllables in words that are stressed naturally in speech.

- *Does it rhyme?* The rhymes of a poem can create great fun. But as an interpreter, usually you do not need to stress the rhymes. If you read to get across the meaning, the rhymes should simply fall into place.

- *How about emphasis?* Some poems seem to call for a fairly even pace and emphasis throughout, like a walk through a park. Others may call for changes in volume or strength to stress words, ideas, or images, like a game of tag. You can use loudness to emphasize words. You can use a strong voice to emphasize words. You can even use silence. If you pause before or after a word, that can emphasize it too.

- *How can you phrase to express the meaning of the poem?* To **phrase** means to group words together. You should group words together so they are easier to understand. You *don't* have to pause at the end of each line. In fact, it may destroy the meaning if you try to do so. Experiment with different phrasings. Read for the punctuation, if that is helpful. Otherwise, read for the ideas.

YOUR PERFORMANCE

Think about things good storytellers do to hold their audiences' attention. You can do those things when you interpret poetry.

Practice your interpretation aloud several times before you perform it. If possible, practice in front of a mirror. You might also ask a classmate or family member to give you helpful feedback.

Be sure you know how to pronounce every word. Use a dictionary for any word you're not sure of. Practice the difficult words and difficult word combinations until you can say them smoothly without stumbling.

Take your time. When you step in front of your audience, don't rush into your performance. Take a few deep breaths and focus on the job you are doing. At the end, pause, look at your audience, and smile, to let them know your performance is finished.

Choral Reading

The word **choral** usually refers to a choir or chorus. In choral reading, it means a small group or a whole class reading aloud together. Sometimes the readers take turns, and sometimes they speak all together. This can be an exciting way to explore a poem with a wide variety of voices.

THE SCRIPT

First you need to decide who reads what lines. Decide how many solo voices you will use and how you are going to group the other voices (all boys, all girls, chorus 1, chorus 2, and so on). Then divide the lines among the available voices. Remember that a single voice or a combination of voices or the whole group might read a single line—or a single word. A director or a group of two or three readers can write the script to assign each line to an individual voice or a combination of voices.

Use your imagination here. You know voices can sing or hum; they can sound happy or sad; they can sound like animals or machines or like wind through the trees. Think about what special sound effects would work for your poem. Then think about how to create those sounds with your voices.

REHEARSAL AND PERFORMANCE

To give a good choral performance you must rehearse. If possible, have a director who signals individuals and groups when to come in. If there is no director, assign one strong reader to start off each choral section so that the rest of the group can come in immediately. You want to give the impression that all voices start and stop together.

Plan your entrances and exits. Also plan where all the people stand or sit when they are not reading. Remember, even when you are not the one reading, you are still onstage. You must do your part to direct the audience's attention by keeping your focus on the ones who are reading.

Make eye contact with your audience. You don't have to memorize the poem you are reading. You should be familiar enough with it, though, that you can look up from your paper from time to time.

Be sure to speak loudly enough. You need to be heard all around the room—including the back row.

Unit 1 Living and Learning

Money Poem

Anonymous

Penny, penny, easily spent,
Copper brown and worth one cent.
Nickel, nickel, thick and fat,
You're worth five cents, I know that.
Dime, dime, little and thin,
I remember—you're worth ten.
Quarter, quarter, big and bold,
You're worth twenty-five, I am told.
Half a dollar, half a dollar,
Giant size.
Fifty cents to buy some fries.
Dollar, dollar, green and long,
With one hundred cents you can't go wrong.

Unit 1 Living and Learning

Lunch Money
by Carol Diggery Shields

Don't ask Dad—he never has any.
Grandma's purse has a nickel and a penny.
Mom has a five, but the car needs gas.
Here's a dirty quarter someone found in the grass.
Checked all our pockets—nothing but gum.
Piggy bank, piggy bank, here I come!

How to Eat a Sandwich Cookie
by Beverly McLoughland

A rookie
Cookie eater
Eats a sandwich cookie
Fast—
1 bite, 2 bite—
End of cookie

A pro
Makes a sandwich cookie
Last—
Knows the art
Of getting to the cookie's
Heart—
Slides the halves
Apart—
Ver-y
Ver-y
Slowly,
Bottom
Against top.
Stops.

Turns the top side
Over. . . .
Yes!
One round and creamy
Sugar moon.

Of course
A pro *always* eats
The blank side
First—
And then,
With a silly grin,
And a thank you
Very much—

Eats the half
That holds
The soft vanilla
Moon.

Meeting the Snake
by Tony Mitton

I used to fear you,
slithery snake,
the way you move,
the shapes you make.

But now I've met you
at the zoo,
I've changed the way
I think of you.

I used to think you
slippy, sly.
And yet I find you
clean and dry,

and soft and slow
and good to touch.
So now I do not fear you,
much.

The Porcupine
by Karla Kuskin

A porcupine looks somewhat silly,
He also is extremely quilly
And if he shoots a quill at you
Run fast
Or you'll be quilly too.
I would not want a porcupine
To be my loving valentine.

Unit 3 People and Nature

Good Morning

by Muriel Sipe

One day I saw a downy duck,
With feathers on his back;
I said, "Good morning, downy duck,"
And he said, "Quack, quack, quack."

One day I saw a timid mouse,
He was so shy and meek;
I said, "Good morning, timid mouse,"
And he said, "Squeak, squeak, squeak."

One day I saw a curly dog,
I met him with a bow;
I said, "Good morning, curly dog,"
And he said, "Bow-wow-wow."

One day I saw a scarlet bird,
He woke me from my sleep;
I said, "Good morning, scarlet bird,"
And he said, "Cheep, cheep, cheep."

I Like Myself!
by Karen Beaumont

I like Myself!
I'm glad I'm me.
There's no one else
I'd rather be.

I like my eyes, my ears, my nose.
I like my fingers and my toes.
I like me wild.
I like me tame.
I like me different
and the same.

I like me fast. I like me slow.
I like me everywhere I go.
I like me on the inside, too,
For all I think and say and do.
Inside, outside, upside down,
from head to toe and all around,
I like it all! It all is me!
And me is all I want to be.
And I don't care in any way
what someone else may think or say.
I may be called a silly nut
or crazy cuckoo bird—so what?

(continued on the next page)

I Like Myself!

(continued)

I am having too much fun, you see,

for anything to bother me!

Even when I look a mess,

I still don't like me any less,

'cause nothing in this world, you know,

can change what's deep inside, and so . . .

No matter if they stop and stare,

no person

ever

anywhere

can make me feel that what they see

is all there really is to me.

I'd *still* like me with fleas or warts

or with a silly snout that snorts,

or knobby knees or hippo hips

or purple polka-dotted lips,

or beaver breath or stinky toes

or horns protruding from my nose,

or—yikes!—with spikes all down my spine,

or hair that's like a porcupine.

I *still* would be the same, you see . . .

I like myself because I'm ME!

Foreign Fare
by Nikki Grimes

Grandma's cooking
Shows off her Southern side:
Yams, crab cakes, mustard greens—
The kind of food I'm used to.
Then she'll go and add
Some foreigner to the bunch.
Today it's Swedish herring.
"Taste it," she says,
Passing me the plate.
The strips of fish swim raw
And silvery in pickle juices
That wrinkle my nose
With suspicion.
"Smells funny," I mumble.
"Humph!" says Grandma.
"You young folks just
Don't know what's good."

Her eyes dare me
To give the fish a try.
I sneer, on cue,
Stab a teensy scrap
And take a bite.
"Hey! This is good," I say,
Surviving the adventure.
Grandma winks at me.
"See? If you only stick
With what you know,
You miss out in life."
"Yeah, well," I shoot back,
"Looks like you got
That problem licked.
Thanks to you, my taste buds
Are gonna see the world."

Unit 6 Freedom

A Lion
by Langston Hughes

A lion in a zoo,
Shut up in a cage,
Lives a life
Of smothered rage.

A lion in the plain,
Roaming free,
Is happy as ever
A lion can be.

Freedom Is . . .
by Claire Grierson

Like a leaf blowing freely,
   Like a bike doing a wheelie.
Like a fish swimming a stream,
   Like a gymnast on a beam.
Like a hawk soaring through the air,
   Like a big wheel at the fair.
Like a cat chasing its tail,
   Like the wind, rain, and hail.
Like a kite up in the sky,
   Like a bee zooming by.
Like a flower soaking up the sun,
    Like a toddler having fun.

Tests About Poetry

Multiple-Choice Test

When you take a multiple-choice test, you can think about the choices to be sure that you choose the best ones. Read the poem and then answer the questions that follow in the left column. Then, in the right column, read some ways you might think about the choices in questions 1–4.

At the Library
by Nikki Grimes

I flip the pages of a book and slip inside,
where crystal seas await and pirates hide.
I find a paradise where birds can talk,
where children fly and trees prefer to walk.
Sometimes I end up on a city street.
I recognize the brownskin girl I meet.
She's skinny, but she's strong, and brave, and wise.
I smile because I see me in her eyes.

Test Question

1. *Crystal seas and paradise where birds can talk,* are examples of which of these?

   A onomatopoeia
   B idiom
   C repetition
   D imagery

Answering the Question

Question 1 There aren't any words that sound like their meanings, so answer A is not correct. These are not familiar phrases or expressions, so answer B is not correct. There isn't a pattern of repeated sounds in these words, so C is not the best answer. The sensory words do help the reader to see and experience the images, so D is the best answer.

Test Question

Answering the Question

2. *Trees prefer to walk* is an example of which of these?

A personification

B comparison

C realism

D same beginning sounds

Question 2 There is no comparison in the phrase, so answer *B* cannot be correct. It is not realistic to have trees that walk, so answer *C* cannot be correct. And there are no beginning sounds that are the same, so answer *D* cannot be correct. When the speaker says that trees walk, she is making something that is not human seem like a human. This is an example of personification, so answer *A* is correct.

3. Based on the way the speaker responds to the *brownskin girl*, what conclusion can you draw about how she feels about herself?

A The speaker sees herself as strong, brave, and wise.

B The speaker wants to live in the city.

C The speaker feels weak and afraid.

D The speaker needs to get some real friends.

Question 3 The speaker doesn't talk about wanting to live anywhere in particular, so *B* is not correct. The speaker doesn't seem to show weakness or fear, so *C* is not correct. We can't say that the speaker doesn't have friends just because she reads in the library, so *D* is not a good answer. But the speaker smiles when she recognizes that she has many of the same characteristics as the brownskin girl, so *A* is the best answer.

4. What does the speaker mean by *Sometimes I end up on a city street?*

A The library is located on a city street.

B The speaker is sorry to have to leave the library.

C A city street is one place that you can read about.

D The speaker would rather read about magical places.

Question 4 The speaker is talking about places she reads about, so *A* is not correct. The speaker doesn't talk about leaving the library, so *B* is not correct. Also, the speaker seems to enjoy reading all types of books, so *D* is not the best answer. When the speaker says she ends up on a city street, she is talking about one of the places she is reading about, so *C* is the best answer.

Writing Test

Read the poem and then follow the directions to write your responses. When you write answers to a test question, you can think about your answers to be sure that they express your understanding. In the right column are some ways you might think about questions 5–7. (Some answers have been filled in as examples.)

My Brother Is as Generous as Anyone Could Be

by Jack Prelutsky

My Brother is as generous
as anyone could be,
for everything he's ever had
he's always shared with me.
He has loaned me his binoculars,
his new computer games,
and his wind-up walking dragon
that breathes artificial flames.

I've been grateful for his robots,
for his giant teddy bear,
but for certain other things
I'd hoped he'd never share—
Though I'm glad he's shared his rockets
And his magic jumping rocks,
I wish my brother hadn't shared
his case of chicken pox.

Test Question

5. List the good and bad things that the brother shares.

Good things shared
binoculars, computer games, dragon, robots, teddy bear

Bad things shared
chicken pox

Answering the Question

Question 5 Have you included all the good things the speaker mentions? Have you included all the bad things? Be prepared to explain why you have labeled something good or bad.

Answering the Question

6. What words does the speaker use to describe how he feels about the things the brother has shared?

> grateful, glad, wish he hadn't

Question 6 Does the speaker feel the same way about everything the brother has shared? How can you tell? What causes the difference in the ways that the speaker feels?

7. This poem is mainly a long list of things the brother is generous about. Write a few sentences to explain how the speaker feels about the brother's generosity and why.

In your answer, be sure that you

- include the bad as well as the good

- explain why the good things are good and the bad things are bad

- explain the two meanings of the word *share*

- support your statements with details from the poem

Question 7 Read the question carefully to be sure you understand what you are to write. How does the tone reveal the speaker's feelings? This question also provides a checklist for you to be sure your answer is a complete one. After you have written your answer, be sure to check it against the list.